AF620026

THE LITTLE TURTLE

And

OTHER STORIES

ISBN 978-1-4716-6140-2

THE LITTLE TURTLE

AND OTHER STORIES

Fiona Stevenson

DEDICATION

This story is dedicated to the friends whose names I have borrowed, because I love them.

DISCLAIMER

No character or event portrayed in the story is based on any person or event that I know or have experienced.

CONTENTS

THE LITTLE TURTLE

Mrs. Tarka and Mrs. Dolly were neighbours. They lived across the hall from one another in a large block of home units. When they saw each other they smiled, said hello, and sometimes had a little chat, as neighbours often do. Mrs. Tarka knew that Mrs. Dolly lived alone with her daughter Miss Penny, and that she had other children who were married and lived far away; also that her husband had died several years earlier. Mrs. Tarka and her husband had four children, all school age but under teenage, who sometimes had pets for longer or shorter periods of time. One of these pets was Thomas, who had once been a pretty, playful little kitten, but was now a very big, very lazy cat, who took up all Mr. Tarka's spare time using him as a groom-cum-armchair.

(How many people have armchairs that stroke them and scratch their ears for them?)

Mr. and Mrs. Tarka were kindly people and good neighbours, and they lived quiet, uneventful lives in a mostly happy sort of way. This does not mean that they were never upset, or that they never had worries or troubles, because they did, just as everyone does. Usually they got over them, or worked them out, as most people seem to do. The children were average children, busy with their schoolwork, their sports, their hobbies; and because they were well taught by their parents, they were usually polite and kindly, too. Sometimes they squabbled, and sometimes they even quarrelled with one another, but because they were really good friends with one another these problems were quickly resolved.

Sometimes Mr. and Mrs. Tarka had a disagreement: and Mr. Tarka's eyebrows would come down in the middle, and the corners of his mouth would come down at the sides, and his nose seemed to jut out a little more than usual. Mrs. Tarka's mouth would go flat and tight, and her eyes would narrow into slits. At these times they were very silent, and the children became quieter and everyone just got on with what they had to do, and no-one said very much at all. (Of course it is not easy to talk with the corners of your mouth turned down, or with your mouth held flat and tight, as you would find if you tried it. But it is very uncomfortable to stay like that for very long, as you would also find if you tried it.) So it wouldn't be very long before Mr. and Mrs. Tarka's mouths, eyes and eyebrows would gradually return to normal, and so would everything else.

On the day that our story begins, Mrs. Dolly was just coming in from her shopping when she saw Mrs. Tarka looking quite upset, hurrying up the stairs to her unit. Mrs. Dolly could see that she was a little bit cross, a little bit sad, and very flustered. This was most unusual, so Mrs. Dolly asked anxiously, "Is there something I can help you with?"

"Oh, dear," said Mrs. Tarka worriedly, "I really don't know what to do. It's this little turtle Ainslie brought home. There isn't anywhere to keep it. I put it into the old fish bowl, but Thomas won't leave it alone – he keeps tipping it over, and I haven't anywhere safe to put it. I just don't know what to do. I think I shall have to flush it down the toilet!" she added unhappily.

Mrs. Dolly was startled. "Is it dead?" she asked.

“No, no.” Mrs. Tarka wrung her hands. “But it soon will be if Thomas gets it. I have been doing nothing all morning but trying to keep it away from him. I just don’t know what else to do!”

Mrs. Dolly shifted her bags slightly. “I don’t think that is a good idea,” she said. “You don’t know if it will go to heaven. Just wait a minute.” She popped her key into the lock and ran into her unit, coming back quite quickly with a little book in her hand.

“Mrs. Tarka, before you flush the little turtle down the toilet please will you read something from my little book so that it will know how to get to heaven – all the bits marked in yellow – you will have to read slowly and carefully to be sure that the turtle understands.”

She thrust the little book into Mrs. Tarka’s hands and went back into her unit.

Just then the surprised Mrs. Tarka heard a splashing crash and hurried into her home to once more rescue the small turtle from Thomas.

A short time later, having mopped up yet another bowl of water, Mrs. Tarka stood at the kitchen sink, watching the little turtle swimming unconcernedly, and opened the little book.

Now I don't know how you would feel about reading to a turtle while it swam in a kitchen sink, but I think I would feel pretty silly. It did not seem to worry Mrs. Tarka, but perhaps that was because she was more worried about flushing the little creature down the toilet!

Slowly and carefully she began to read the bits marked yellow in the book, keeping one eye on the little turtle to make sure it understood. Sometimes just to be quite sure, she read a bit twice, and once she stopped and read that portion three times very thoughtfully. Then she closed the book, sat down slowly on her kitchen stool and gazed into the sink with unseeing eyes. Sometimes her lips moved as though she was repeating the words to herself, and she looked a little puzzled and a little wondering, as if she could see something in the sink that she could not understand at all.

She wasn't sure how long she sat there before she heard a tap at her door, and Miss Penny came in with a cup of tea and a plate of sandwiches. "Mummy thought you might like a cup of tea," explained Miss Penny.

"Thank you. Thank you." Mrs. Tarka was still distracted. "Can you explain something to me, Miss Penny? I don't understand this at all..." And she held out the book Mrs. Dolly had given her, opened. Miss Penny read out the bit that she pointed at: "...the whole creation groans and is in pain together with us until we receive the adoption, the salvation that God has purchased for us when Jesus Christ died on the cross at Calvary."

"What does that mean?" asked Mrs. Tarka again. "What does it mean?"

"Mrs. Tarka," said Miss Penny carefully, "Do you know the Bible story at all?"

"I think so," replied Mrs. Tarka helplessly, "I mean, a little bit ... not very much. It is such a big book, I couldn't read it all, but I have read the children Bible stories from their Bible storybooks. But that is all history, isn't it? It's about things that happened years and years ago."

"Yes," said Miss Penny. "It is a big book. It is history, and it is about things that happened years and years ago. But it is much more than that."

And she went on to explain to Mrs. Tarka how that God had created the world and everything in it; how that man had sinned and spoiled the whole of creation, bringing trouble, pain and sickness as the results of sin, not only to man but to everything that God had created; and how that God, through His Son, Jesus Christ, had made a way for man to become free from sin and to once more become a child of God, and how that there will one day be a time when Jesus will again rule the whole creation, but until that time all of creation will have pain and trouble.

"But that isn't fair," protested Mrs. Tarka. "Why would God let everything suffer because of man?"

“It wouldn’t be fair,” agreed Miss Penny, “except God gave His creation to man. Man was given this whole world to enjoy it and to care for it. But he spoiled it. God has done everything He could, and the rest is up to us.”

“What do you mean – the rest is up to us? What can we do – how can we change anything?” Mrs. Tarka sounded quite indignant.

“Well,” explained Miss Penny, “if we really believe what the Bible tells us about God, Who is the Creator and Who is totally good; and about man and how he sinned and was separated from God; and if we really believe what the Bible tells us about Jesus Christ – about His birth, His death and His resurrection; if we really believe what Jesus told Nicodemus: that God loved the world so much that He sent His only Son so that everyone who believes in Him would not be condemned (die because of sin), but would have everlasting life; - if we really believe these things then we can ask God for His forgiveness and He will make us His children again. When we do that, and we begin to live the sort of life that He always wanted us to live, we begin to affect the other parts of creation too. And then we will make a difference to everyone and everything that is close to us, and when people close to us learn about what Jesus has done for us and they do the same thing we did – believe and ask God for forgiveness – we start a ripple effect growing, and, well, you see what happens, don't you?"

"I think so," answered Mrs. Tarka, "but it is so hard to understand why God should bother with us. Why didn't He just blot everything out and start again?"

"Because He loves us, you goose!" laughed Miss Penny, hugging Mrs. Tarka impulsively. "Here you are, trying to think of some way to manage the little turtle rather than flushing it down the toilet and you wonder about God! And you didn't even make the turtle! And by the way, I can help you with the turtle, too," she added triumphantly.

"Can you? How?"

“I work at the museum,” explained Miss Penny, “and sometimes the zoos and the big aquariums send us dead specimens to mount and display. I can send them a live specimen in return! I am quite sure that the big aquarium will be able to find him a home.” She stroked the back of the little turtle with a gentle finger.

“That would be wonderful!” exclaimed Mrs. Tarka, and then she added hesitantly, “Will you help me to tell God that I do believe what you have explained to me about Him, about the Bible and about Jesus Christ? I need to ask Him to forgive me too, and I want to find out how I can learn more about the kind of life He wants me to live, and how to help His creation not to suffer so much.”

The last I heard of the little turtle it was growing bigger and swimming strongly, and Miss Penny tells me that is because Mrs. Tarka has not forgotten to pray for it every day, and to thank God for the little turtle that was the reason she heard about the love of God.

MISS PENNY AND PROFESSOR ROLEY

I called to see Professor Roley at the museum. Putting aside his work with a little sigh, he flipped his intercom and asked Miss Penny to bring two cups of tea to the courtyard, after which he led me to a shady seat beside a sun-drenched lawn.

I watched my friend as he stretched his legs and leaned back, his eyes closed. He looked so very tired and I wondered if there was any better news of his father who had already been in hospital for several days. While I was thinking about it he answered my thoughts.

"No." He said. "He hasn't come out of the coma. The doctors are still not sure what the cause is. They are afraid that if he does come round he will be permanently brain-damaged."

I was silent, not sure if I should sympathize or try to cheer him up. And how do you cheer someone up when the news is so bad?

Professor Roley's father was a quiet, gentle man in his late seventies. He spent much of his time pottering around at the museum, cleaning treasures, doing minor repairs, and loving the gardens to bright and glorious blossom.

The silence was still unbroken when Miss Penny came out with a small wheeled tray of tea. She greeted me with a pleasant smile and enquired whether Professor Roley wished her to confirm an appointment. I saw she had added a dainty plate of sandwiches to his order. I poured while they discussed the appointment and when Miss Penny had gone I passed his cup and offered him a sandwich. He smiled as he took one.

"Bless Miss Penny. She is quite sure we will all starve ourselves to death, although I don't think there is anyone more concerned about Jacko than she is."

(Jacko was everyone's favourite name for Professor Roley's father.)

"She fairly haunts the hospital," he went on, "and half the museum garden is in his room. She pops in at least three times a day to pray for him, and I believe her mother has organised with some of her friends to pray the whole twenty-four hours of the day, until he is well again."

He was silent for a few minutes before continuing. "I don't quite know what to think about all this. I believe there is a God – or something." He waved his hand vaguely. "I mean, all of this – it's so organised, so detailed, there must be some sort of intelligence behind it, but I gather Miss Penny and her mother have a different conception of God. They seem to believe that not only is there a Creator, but that He is a personality, and that He has a moment by moment interest in every creature and in every event that takes place. At least, I think that's how it is." He ended uncertainly. "I don't think I could believe that."

There was a wistful note in his voice. I thought of Miss Penny and her mother, Mrs. Dolly. Over a period of some years I had come to know them quite well, and I knew that this was a fairly good description of their belief in God. They believed quite simply that God had created this great, diverse and wonderful universe; had planted and peopled the earth and given it to man. They believed that man had spoiled God's first plan, breaking the only rule that God had given; and they believed that God Himself had provided a way in which men and women individually could find their way back to friendship with Him. And I know that for them He was not just a Friend. To talk about God was as natural as breathing. To talk to God was instinctive – He was always right there with them.

"I know." I said gravely. "I don't know many people who share quite the same simple belief they have. Most of us have a lot more 'if's and buts'' about what we believe. But basically, I think they are quite right. I mean," hesitating, trying to think clearly, "God is not just a force. He is a personality. And He does have an interest in every part of His creation. That is why it is right for us to pray for one another, and about our problems, and ... and things." I ended lamely as I watched the frown deepen on my friend's face.

"There's not much logic about it," my friend disagreed shortly. "I mean, you want rain because everything is so dry, but Peter down the road has a tennis match on so he prays for a dry day. It stands to reason there will be conflicting interests. How is God to satisfy all of you?"

I tried not to smile. "Perhaps that is true, but there are times when our interests do not conflict ..."

Professor Roley 'heard' my thoughts again and interrupted me harshly.

"Yes, they do. I happen to know that some people are praying that Jacko will just die peacefully without regaining consciousness, while others are praying that he will not only come out of the coma, but he will be restored to normal health. Quite apart from the fact that that is medically impossible, you have to admit that there is a conflict of interests there."

I winced at the pain in his voice and the misery in his eyes while I tried to find words to comfort him. Neither of us had noticed Miss Penny who had come out with a message in her hand. Now she knelt beside Professor Roley's chair and put a hand on his arm.

"Professor Roley," she said softly, "it is not a conflict of interests. None of us want Jacko to go on as he is. None of us want to see you worrying so much. Our interest is the same. The only difference is in what we believe God is able to do." She paused, then added: "Dr. Gerry has rung from the hospital. He would like you to go up right away. Professor Don has his car waiting for you out front."

Professor Roley seemed frozen into immobility. The fear of bad news and the unreasoning hope of good news combined with an inability to decide which would be which, sapped his strength and locked him into his chair.

Miss Penny stood up and offered him her hand with a charming smile. "Come on, Professor Roley. You needn't be afraid. Even if you aren't quite sure of God, I know how good He is and how much He loves you and Jacko. Jacko knows too, - we were talking about it only a day or so before he went into hospital, and he told me that one day he would just walk out of this world and into God's presence, and that would be the most wonderful thing of all. Well, he wasn't walking when they took him to hospital, was he?"

Like a sleep-walker Professor Roley shook his head, rose and followed her. As they walked I pulled the tea-tray behind them, half listening to Miss Penny confidently arranging to take Professor Roley's car home and to feed the Professor's cats.

I pushed the little tray into the kitchen and stepped out of the front door, my mind a jumble of unfinished thoughts and prayers. Miss Penny stood on the steps watching Professor Don drive away. I heard her say softly, "Go with God, Professor Roley, go with God."

MR. JACKO

I expect you are wondering what happened to Mr. Jacko, Professor Roley and Miss Penny. Before I tell you that I think I should tell you something more about Mr. Jacko.

Mr. Jacko was an elderly man when I first met him, retired, and a widower. He helped with the garden at the museum, and now and then he did little maintenance jobs for Professor Roley.

I had been introduced to him and had spoken to him a few times on one or another visit to the museum. Then one day when I dropped off a parcel for Miss Penny I met Mr. Jacko as I was leaving. He stopped me with a question.

"Would you like a cup of tea?"

I was just about to excuse myself when I saw the wistfulness in his eyes and decided that I would like nothing better. We filled up a tray in the kitchen and took ourselves to the rose garden. The day was warm but we found a shaded corner and settled ourselves comfortably. I poured the tea, Mr. Jacko passed the cookies, and for a while we sipped and munched in companionable silence.

Then Mr. Jacko put down his cup with a sigh, and wiped some crumbs from his moustache with a large, white handkerchief.

"Its seven years today since I lost Margery, and it was all my fault."

He sounded so lost and lonely and I didn't know what to say. But I needn't have worried – after a little he went on:

"I wasn't a Christian, you know. Margery was. When I was away at the war she prayed for us. Everyone she knew or heard of being at the front, she prayed for us. I didn't think it was much good, but it didn't do us any harm and it kept her happy. Anyway, I wasn't there to stop her."

He paused for a while. I waited.

"When I came home from the war we picked up our lives again and things just went on. Margery went to church, and sometimes she asked me to go with her. I went now and then – if there was a special occasion, weddings, christenings, Christmas – you know. She still prayed for every man and his dog. As long as she didn't bother me with her prayers I didn't mind. She was a good woman. Kind-hearted."

He paused again, looking back at the memories of his wife.

"One evening on my way home I stopped with some friends for a beer. Margery didn't like it but she never said too much. Traffic was heavy at that time and she was concerned for my safety. Well, we got to talking about the war and what with one thing and another time went by and we had several beers – more than usual. Then one of the fellows noticed how long we had been at it, so we broke it up and all went home.

"Well by this time Margery was nearly out of her mind with worry. When she heard the car turn into the drive she ran out of the house. I think she thought I had been in an accident and someone was coming to tell her the bad news. She was often afraid of that, you know. I was driving too fast, and I misjudged the turn. First thing I knew, Margie was lying in a heap and the car was half onto the veranda. She was unconscious. I picked her up into the car and rushed as fast as I could to the hospital. I didn't know what to do. I didn't know who to go to for help. The nurses were wonderful."

Mr. Jacko paused again. He was very still. His eyes looked far away back, through many years of memories.

I filled the teacups again and tried not to notice the tears on his cheeks.

"It was several days before she regained consciousness. They held out very little hope, but one day she opened her eyes and looked at me. "Hello, Jacko," she said very softly, and held out her hand. I wanted to tell her how sorry I was, how glad she was back, but I couldn't speak. Before I could say anything she spoke again, and her voice was stronger. "I am going home to Jesus, Jacko. He's waiting for me now. But I wanted you to know that I love you. I wanted to pray for you one more time. Jacko, I know that you didn't mean to hurt me, I know that you are sorry. Thank you, my dear, I accept that. What hurts me so much more is that you are not a Christian, so this is probably goodbye forever. I know that you think religion is for women and children, but being a Christian is different to religion. So my last prayer for you is that you will ask Jesus for His forgiveness." Those were her last words."

After a while he went on, "I asked Him, you know, several times. I was sorry for myself. I was angry. I was bitter. So I asked Him; I begged Him and I shouted at Him. But nothing happened. I just got more sorry for myself, more angry, more bitter. Then one evening Pastor Bert came around. He had picked up a book Margery had lent him, thought about how often he and his wife had prayed with Margery, and decided to come and see me. To cut a long story a little shorter, he explained a lot of things to me, so that at last I understood that it was no good asking Jesus to forgive me just because I felt sorry for myself, or angry or bitter. At last I understood why Margery said that being a Christian was different to being religious. And at last I began to understand who Jesus is and why I should ask Him for forgiveness."

Mr. Jacko turned to me with a very sweet smile, and I saw that he had come back to the present day.

"Thank you for listening to an old man. Now I can remember Margery with gladness. I know I will see her again quite soon. But now it is my turn to pray. Now I pray for my son who thinks religion is for old men ..."

He gave me a mischievous grin. "But we know, you and I, that being a Christian is not the same as religion, and that we all need to know who Jesus is, and that we each of us need his forgiveness."

I thought about all of this while I was praying for Mr. Jacko after he went to hospital and I thought you might like to know too. So I have told you.

PROFESSOR ROLEY

Perhaps I should tell you more about Professor Roley, Mr. Jacko's son. He was one of the Directors of a Museum. Not a very large museum, but also not a small museum. If you have visited a museum you will be aware that they usually display dead things and sometimes very old things.

When I was a child my father often took us to the museum to look at the animals – a treat that my brother and I enjoyed greatly. But we didn't learn very much other than to recognise certain of the animal species, and it was only after I grew older that I realised how much information was available to students and other interested persons. The information didn't relate only to animal, bird or insect life. There were also sections dealing with civilisations, like the Incas of Peru, with minerals, or with the natural ecological systems.

When we first met Professor Roley he had a special interest in the fish of the Southern Hemisphere. His office was not big enough to keep in it all the notes, photographs and reports that he had collected about the different kinds of fish, their names, their habitat, and their life cycle generally. Over the five or six years that he had been studying these fish he had also received specimens from other researchers. Some of them were live specimens, shipped in especially built tanks. Many were dead specimens, frozen or preserved in a special fluid. Others were skeletons, or parts of skeletons, carefully packed to prevent them breaking in transit. Many of the dead specimens and skeletons were displayed in the museum. Later, when the museum was reorganised and enlarged, tanks were put in so that live fish could also be displayed.

In between research trips, Professor Roley maintained the fish displays. From time to time older displays were removed, making way for a specimen recently received to be put in place. It seemed there was always something more to see or learn about.

In his work, Professor Roley had a great deal of reading to do: books, letters and reports. And he had to write reports himself, and answer the many letters he received. Some people thought that he wasn't very friendly because he was a quiet man and often withdrawn, especially when he was puzzling out a problem, when he found it hard to concentrate on a conversation. Outside of his work, his interests were his cats and music, and even they took second place to his work!

However, this thin, silent man had a great many friends. Although he wasn't chatty, he was kind and courteous, and just as he remembered the books he read, so he remembered the people he met.

"Tell young Ben to come and see me," he'd say to the mechanic when he stopped for petrol. "I think I have found what he was looking for."

And when young Ben came, their two heads would dip low over young Ben's latest project, hands busy, voices mingling, occasionally a young laugh or a dry chuckle, and when young Ben left he had a smile a mile wide, and a friendly wave for everyone.

Or he would stop off at the corner store to buy some milk or fish for the cats. "For Susan," and he would pass a small parcel across to Susan's mother, who put the package behind her or under the counter, saying, "She had a good day today, and did some more work on her painting," or "A lot of pain today. The Physio is with her." And he would smile or nod sadly. In this way they shared the knowledge that Susan was precious and important to both of them, and without saying or doing anything more, they comforted each other in their sharing.

My husband is a botanist, and in the course of his research he was introduced to Professor Roley. A firm friendship was formed when they spent time in the same area, each researching his own interest, each able to provide information to the other. Then they discovered that they shared another interest – music. And I discovered that an old friend – Miss Penny – worked at the museum.

From Miss Penny I learned that Professor Roley lived in a "time capsule": past time was only of interest when it directly influenced some part of today; future time did not exist until it became today. Professor Roley believed that speculation about either the past or the future was a waste of time. What was important was what we needed to know and do today.

Miss Penny smiled when she told me this, and I knew why. Miss Penny lives in a very three-dimensional time: her yesterdays and tomorrows all muddled into her todays! As she explained to me, “Our today is tomorrow for all those people still living in yesterday on the - other side of the world!”

She corresponds with, and prays for people in many different parts of the world. She says that we have time but God doesn’t, and for Someone who has the longest ever day He has the greatest ever patience, and before His today is over Professor Roley will have found yesterday, tomorrow and the love of God! “Because,” she says, “so many people are praying for him – and,” with a laugh, “God always gets His man!”

MR. JACKO GOES HOME

"Miss Penny? Miss Penny?"

His voice was so soft that Miss Penny wasn't sure if he had really spoken. She moved quickly to the bed and asked, "Did you call me, Mr. Jacko?"

His eyes were open. "Miss Penny, will you please ring for the Sister and then 'phone Professor Roley? I need to see him."

"Of course I will." Miss Penny reached for the bell. "Shall I give him any other message?"

"Just tell him I'm back!" Mr. Jacko gave her a small smile. "Don't want him to panic."

The nursing Sister came in and Miss Penny went down to the public telephone boxes. When she returned to the ward she found the nursing Sister crossly telling Mr. Jacko that he was a stubborn old man! Turning to Miss Penny she explained that Mr. Jacko insisted on getting up and getting dressed, and then walking down to the hospital entrance to meet Professor Roley. All this while she was tying his shoelaces and helping him to stand.

“Miss Penny will help me,” explained Mr. Jacko patiently. “May I have your arm please, Miss Penny?”

He put his frail hand lightly on her arm and they walked slowly out of the small private ward and across to the lifts. As they walked the long corridor to the entrance he seemed to gain strength. At the door he stopped and straightened himself, lifting his hand from Miss Penny’s arm.

“Thank you, Miss Penny,” he said as they stepped out onto the driveway leading to the parking area. “I will go ahead to meet Roley. Will you please wait for us here?”

He walked ahead, straight and steady, but slowly. Miss Penny was relieved to see Professor Roley coming toward them.

Father and son met and spoke briefly before turning back to Miss Penny. When they reached her Mr. Jacko said firmly, “We will go into the cafeteria for a cup of tea, and then we will go back up to the ward.”

He turned to Miss Penny. “I am going home this afternoon, my dear, and there are matters I must discuss with my son. I would be very grateful if you would stay nearby – perhaps the balcony – and pray for us.”

Professor Roley started to protest, but Mr. Jacko silenced him with a shake of his head. “Come.”

When they had had their tea and settled themselves back in the ward, Miss Penny slipped out to the balcony, softly closing the door behind her. She leaned on the balcony wall and looked across the nearby buildings to the flowering trees in the park. How pretty they were. She thought of Mr. Jacko's words, "I am going home this afternoon" and a deep grief swelled inside. She prayed. She knew what Mr. Jacko would be telling Professor Roley and she mourned for the parting of father and son, both so dear to each other and to her. She prayed.

She saw and heard nothing more until Professor Roley opened the door and called to her. Her face and hands were wet with tears and she gave them a quick scrub with a damp handkerchief before going in.

Mr. Jacko looked a little tired as he relaxed in the armchair beside the bed. "Yes, yes I am ready," he murmured, but he wasn't talking to them. He reached for the bell and pressed the buzzer. Professor Roley and Miss Penny stood before him like two small children, waiting. The nursing Sister came in quietly behind them. Mr. Jacko stood and embraced first Professor Roley and then Miss Penny.

"Goodbye, my son." He shook his hand.

“Till we meet again, my daughter.” His frail hand lightly brushed her cheek.

“Thank you, Sister.” And he sat back again, relaxed and smiling slightly.

They looked at each other, and at him. Sister stepped forward and lifted his wrist. “He’s gone,” she said briefly, brushing his eyes closed with a gentle hand. “Take as long as you need.” And she went out, leaving Professor Roley and Miss Penny alone.

For some time they sat without speaking, then Professor Roley looked directly at Miss Penny. His eyes were wet.

“Miss Penny, he called you his daughter. I know that he loved you and looked on you as a daughter. Would you consider ...?”

Miss Penny shook her head and raised a finger to her lips. “No, Professor Roley. This is not the right time. You have too many things to think about, and to do.”

“But if I don’t say it now ...” Professor Roley paused. “How will I know when it is the right time?”

“I will,” promised Miss Penny.

The small church was packed to capacity for Mr. Jacko’s funeral. Professor Roley looked around in surprise. He recognised a number of the people who were there, but there were many who were strangers to him. Near the front of the church he saw Miss Penny with Mrs. Dolly, and in front of them a young boy with a walking cane. An usher escorted him as the chief mourner to a pre-selected seat, but he stopped him with a question, “Please may I sit with Miss Penny and her mother? I know so few people here.”

The usher stopped and looked at him, then nodded and moved away, leaving him with Miss Penny and Mrs. Dolly.

There were rustles and whispers as people seated themselves, until a tall man came forward and stood beside the casket. There was quiet as he raised his hand and said, “Let us pray.”

His prayer for the mourners was brief and simple, extending to them the comfort, love and peace of God.

“Amen.” He looked around the chapel and smiled. “I know that there are many of you who would like to share what Mr. Jacko meant to you – too many for me to allow you all to speak. But there is one young man here who has asked expressly to be able to do so. Dominic.”

He gestured toward the boy with the walking cane, and Dominic came to him, limping and leaning on the cane. The minister turned again to the people.

"Dominic is fourteen years old and has known Mr. Jacko for the last seven of those years. He has a very good reason for wanting to tell you what Mr. Jacko meant to him. Go ahead, Dom." And he returned to his seat.

Dominic nervously cleared his throat. "Mr. Jacko was the best friend I had. I never knew any of my grandparents. They died before I was born. My dad died in an accident before I was seven and I was crippled in the same accident. Even though one leg was not as badly damaged as the other, the doctors were sure I would never walk again. I didn't care. I wished I was dead, too. But one of the nurses thought that one day I would maybe surprise the doctors, and she used to come and talk to me. Sometimes she brought me things to cheer me up, and one day she brought Mr. Jacko.

"After that Mr. Jacko came regularly to visit me. We talked about all sorts of things. He brought books and read to me. He brought me a sketch block and pencils and taught me to draw. He said a boy needed to do things with his hands even if he couldn't walk. He brought me a penknife and some small blocks of wood, and showed me how to carve little things. One day he said to me that since he had no grandchildren and I had no grandparents, what did I think about adopting him as a grandfather. Then one day he was waiting for me when the physiotherapist brought me back to the ward, and he spoke to the therapist for quite a long time. After that he spoke to my mother and the doctor, although I didn't know that at the time. Then he started working on my leg, rubbing it and talking to himself. At least, that is what I thought he was doing. Now I know that he was massaging it, and praying! Sometimes he worked on the good leg too. Until one day he suggested that I should stand on my good leg for a short while each day so that it would get stronger. And then he thought that maybe I could hop on my good leg while he supported me. Sometimes I was ready to give up, but he kept visiting me and encouraging me, and my good leg became stronger. Then he and the therapist brought a brace for my crippled leg, and they helped me to put some weight on that foot too. Gradually, slowly – very slowly – that leg got stronger, too. One day Mr. Jacko brought me a special walking stick and showed me how to use it. It is special because Mr. Jacko made it so that it could 'grow' with me and I wouldn't have to have a new one as I grew taller. This one has grown about four inches since then!

"All the time he was doing this for me he was telling me about God. He read me Bible stories, and stories about missionaries. He taught me songs and explained who Jesus was and what He had done for me. He spoke to my mother too. We both prayed and asked Jesus for forgiveness, and to be made the children of God. When I came out of hospital Mr. Jacko brought us to this church and we have been coming here ever since."

Dominic paused and looked around.

"But that is not all Mr. Jacko did for me. Not long ago we were reading the Bible together and we were reading the part where Jesus told His disciples that He had to go away but He would send them another Comforter. Mr. Jacko closed his Bible and he told me that was happening to him, too. It was nearly time for him to go home. But he said he had prayed for me, too, and God had given him a gift for me, a gift of healing. He explained that sometimes healing was instant, and sometimes it took time. He said that he could not heal, only God can do that, but that God allowed people who believed in Him to bring God's gift of healing to other people, and that God had allowed him to bring a gift of healing to me. But that I was still not entirely healed and it was time for him to go home soon. So he prayed and asked the Holy Ghost, the Comforter, to complete my healing, and to give me gifts of healing for others. He explained that the Holy Ghost would take care of me, and He would never leave me, but that I must be careful to listen to Him and obey Him.

"Just a few days ago I was reading a book Mr. Jacko had left with me. I knew he was in hospital and I put the book down and prayed for him. Somebody came and stood next to me. He said, "Mr. Jacko has gone home, son, just as he told you. I have come as he asked Me to do. If you will walk with Me I will teach you. If you will hear and follow Me I will give you the gifts of healing for others. You will always walk with a limp – you are young and I do not wish you to forget what it means to be crippled. Give Me your hands."

While He was talking His hand rested on my crippled knee, and my knee got very warm with the warmth of His hand. I gave Him my hands and He held them for a short while. My hands got so very warm from his hands, and I started to tremble. Then my hands got cool again and He was gone. And yet, he was still near me, and has been ever since.

For seven years Mr. Jacko was my very best friend. But he introduced me to Jesus who brought me to His Father and made me a member of his family. And now the Comforter, the Holy Ghost, is my constant companion too. If I were to try to thank Mr. Jacko for what he has done for me he would just say, "That's what friends are for."

I don't need the walking cane any more. I am new on the inside because when Mr. Jacko loved me he showed me the love of Jesus, and when I prayed and asked Jesus to forgive me, He made me new. I am new on the outside because Mr. Jacko accepted a gift of healing and brought it to me, and because Mr. Jacko explained to me about the Healer, Jesus, and the Comforter, the Holy Ghost, and prayed for me to understand and listen to them."

Dominic paused. He laid the cane in front of the casket among the flowers and cards. He took a small, flat parcel from his pocket and walked across to Professor Roley.

“This is for you, Professor Roley. I will be praying for you, too.” Dominic returned to his seat.

After the funeral service Professor Roley spent some time speaking with Dominic and the minister. They were all back at the church, sharing cups of tea and talking about Mr. Jacko and what Dominic had told them. Miss Penny sat with an untouched cup at her side, and prayed for her friends.

When everyone was leaving Professor Roley came across to ask Miss Penny and Mrs. Dolly if he might take them home. As they walked towards his car Professor Roley stopped.

“Miss Penny, there is something I want to tell you,” he started. “I have asked Jesus to forgive me and make me a member of His family.”

“I know.” Miss Penny smiled. “And yes, this is the right time. And yes, I will.”

“How did you know?” asked Professor Roley.

“I was praying for you,” was her reply.

MR. JACKO'S LEGACY

Following Mr. Jacko's funeral Professor Roley invited Professor Don and I to share a meal with him and Miss Penny.

"Come early so that we can have a chat beforehand."

So here we were in his office, relaxing and enjoying each other's company. It was several weeks since the funeral, and we were surprised at Professor Roley's acceptance of the loss of his father. He was a very intense man and felt any loss very deeply. I sat back and watched while he and Professor Don discussed and cleared away certain work matters. The late afternoon was cool, and Miss Penny had provided mugs of hot coffee. I held mine in both hands and was comforted by the warmth.

When the men had finished their discussion I asked, "Roley, the last time I was here you were called up to the hospital. What happened at that time?"

Professor Roley pursed his lips, considering before replying. "Apparently Jacko showed some signs of regaining consciousness: he moved slightly and spoke very softly. At one point the doctor thought he heard him say my name, but he couldn't make out anything else that Jacko was saying. This continued intermittently for a period of time, so they sent for me. But when I got there he had relapsed into total unconsciousness again. No-one had an explanation. The doctors were not even sure whether this was a hopeful sign or not. You must remember that Jacko had been in a coma for a very long period of time and there was little hope of a complete recovery. But there were no obvious signs of physical distress and he was breathing quite normally. They had him on a drip-feed only to keep him hydrated and to supply certain nutrients to the body. Miss Penny was there when he finally did come round and he spoke first to her. There were no signs of physical or mental impairment. He was just the Jacko we all knew and loved."

Miss Penny added, "He seemed a little weak at first, but that didn't last long. He would soon have been eighty, you know, and I was surprised at his strength. He had lost a lot of weight during that time. It seems almost unbelievable to me that he was able to walk the distance he did, and so soon."

We had all been at Mr. Jacko's funeral, and for a while we remembered highlights of that day. Although naturally there was the sorrow of loss, it was really a happy day with many people sharing memories of their friendship with Mr. Jacko. He had come into the church only a few years beforehand after the death of his wife, but it wasn't long before he fitted right in and began to take an active part in all the church activities. Even so, it was quite a surprise to find how many people were there because Mr. Jacko had brought them! It just seemed to happen so unobtrusively. I thought of the time he had spent in the gardens and helping out at the museum, and wondered how this elderly man had found the time to do all that he had done.

Professor Roley interrupted my thoughts. "Well now, before we go to dinner, Miss Penny and I have something to ask you."

He looked at her and she inclined her head slightly. He stood up and sat down again, and looked around as if he was expecting something to happen. But nothing did. Professor Don and I looked at each other and wondered what to expect. Then, in a rush:

“Miss Penny and I would like you to assist at our wedding, please.”

This was certainly unexpected.

“Wedding?” we echoed. “You’re getting married?”

The Professor grinned and Miss Penny started to giggle.

“Married.” They said together, “Hitched. Spliced. Wedded.”

Professor Don and I started to laugh. We knew they were good friends. They had worked together for many years, and been comfortable together despite one or two disagreements. But there had been no evidence of any deeper attachment. We knew that Professor Roley had recently started attending the church where Mr. Jacko had been a member, and we had hoped that this would help him in the loss of his father. We knew that Miss Penny and her mother attended the same church – they had been doing so for many years. But this was very sudden and we wanted an explanation.

"What brought this on?"

Professor Roley and Miss Penny looked at each other. "You," she said. Professor Roley turned back to us.

"It was something Mr. Jacko said."

He did not share with us his final discussion with his father, but explained how Mr. Jacko had farewelled each of them.

“He said to me, ‘Goodbye, my son,’ and he sounded quite sad; but to Miss Penny he said, ‘Till we meet again, my daughter,’ and I realised there was something I didn’t understand. But even more than that, I saw Miss Penny as his daughter, and I knew the only way she could be his daughter was if she married me, and that it was important that she should marry me. It was as if I was seeing her through different eyes, and realised how important she was to me and how much I really loved her. But she wouldn’t let me speak, and now I know why.”

He stopped and fingered a small wooden plaque that lay on his desk. “Your turn,” he said to Miss Penny.

“After the funeral ..” she started, stopped and started again.

“Professor Roley was not a Christian,” she said, “and I knew what he was going to say. When you love someone and pray for them you know a lot more about them than they realise. It wasn’t the right time for him to ask me, because I would have had to say no, and that would have hurt him too much, especially as he had just lost his father. But after the funeral, when he was talking to Dom and the minister – I was praying for him then too – I knew what was happening and I knew it would be all right. So I told him so."

She smiled at him fondly. "I wouldn't have believed that someone with so many arguments and so many questions could learn and accept the Scriptures so quickly!"

"It's my teacher." Professor Roley said proudly. "Dominic has been teaching me all that Jacko taught him. He is a very good teacher. And he made this."

He held up the little wooden plaque. It was a beautiful engraved likeness of Mr. Jacko.

"He gave it to me at the funeral," he added almost unnecessarily. We had all seen Dominic hand the small parcel to Professor Roley, but so much had been happening no-one thought about it afterwards.

"Well, will you?" they asked together.

"Yes," said Professor Don, while I asked, "What do you want us to do?"

Miss Penny wanted a matron-of-honour to give her support, and Professor Roley a groomsman to make sure he didn't forget anything. It would just be a small wedding, very quiet, but each felt that they would need support, and Professor Roley especially felt that he needed someone to make sure he wouldn't forget the time and get waylaid. Miss Penny wasn't sure that Professor Don was the right person for that as they tended to get waylaid together, but said she was happy to rely on the Holy Ghost to keep them reminded!

As it was the church was packed with well-wishers and friends. Professor Don gave Miss Penny away and Dominic was the groomsman. He also sang to them from the Song of Solomon:

Rise up, my love, my fair one,

and come away;

For, lo, the winter is past, the rain is over and gone,

the flowers appear on the earth,

the time of the singing of the birds is come

and the voice of the turtle is heard in our land.

The fig tree putteth forth her green figs

and the vines with the tender grapes give a good smell.

Arise, my love, my fair one,

and come away.

The minister reminded them that although they were coming to a 'springtime of marriage in their autumn years' they could expect all the natural seasons to follow, and that in all the changing times and circumstances they needed at all times to remain aware of the presence of the Lord, and of each other's needs.

"You will each have a great sufficiency in the other, but do not exclude those who love you, or those who need you. Bring them into the circle of your warmth, and they will enrich you as you bless them. The Lord has knit you together. He will give your relationship a depth and an increase far beyond your expectations as surely as you follow Him."

He reminded them of God's laws regarding marriage, and the blessings promised in the Scriptures.

They were overwhelmed by the generous goodwill of all the church people, and I, although a member of a sister church, was touched by their spontaneous unity. Professor Don confided to me during the reception luncheon that he had never experienced anything like this before.

"I am not really a church-goer," he said, "but on the few occasions I have attended it always seemed a bit too solemn and not really very happy. But both Mr. Jacko's funeral and this wedding have been more like celebrations." He hesitated, suddenly uncertain. "How can you really celebrate a funeral?" he asked.

Instead of answering his question I asked him, “Professor Don, you’re not a Christian, are you?”

He looked surprised, “Yes I am!” And then he looked at me again. “Or perhaps we are talking about different things. I always thought I was a Christian. What do you mean?”

“Professor Don, a Christian is a person who is committed to, and follows, Christ. If you really do not know very much about Christ, how can you be committed to Him? If you do not know what He is doing or where He is going, how can you follow Him?”

He thought about that for a while before coming back to me. “How can I know Christ in the way that you do?”

For a moment I was nonplussed, but this was a very important question. I took a New Testament from my handbag and opened it at the letter to the Romans.

“First, Don, you must see yourself as God sees you. You are a sinner.”

I pointed to a verse on thc page, handing him the New Testament to read it for himself. I thought he might have difficulty with this because Professor Don is one of the kindest, nicest of men. But he read the Scripture and just said, “I see, now what?”

I tried to keep calm and to remember the best Scriptures to help him to understand that as a sinner he had no place in the family of God, but that God had made a way, through Jesus Christ who said “I am the door.”

Jesus, who was the Son of God, had become a sacrifice on behalf of every person, and died on the cross so that we could be forgiven. I explained that if he, Professor Don, believed that Jesus was the Son of God and accepted His sacrifice, he would be brought into the family of God. If he then committed himself to Jesus and followed Him, he would be a Christian.

After thinking about this, Professor Don asked me, "How do I do this?"

I answered a bit vaguely, "Well, you pray," adding hastily, " – that's just talking to God, you know, telling Him how you feel and asking Him to take control of your life. Tell Him you want Jesus Christ to be your Saviour, and that you want to follow Him from now on. But you have to mean it!"

I ended in a rush, feeling totally inadequate, wondering if anything I had said made sense to poor Professor Don. But Don looked down at his hands resting on the edge of the table, and he didn't notice the hush that fell as he started to speak.

"Lord God, I realise that I am a sinner, and I really don't know anything about you. Please will you take control of my life. Thank you for making a way for me to come to you through Jesus Christ your Son. I need Him to be my Saviour, and I do want to follow Him. Please help me to do this."

"And I do mean it!" He turned to me. "I feel somehow different – sort so clean, and fresh and new. Did you feel like that too?"

Miss Penny leaned across me. "We all did, Professor Don. I am so glad you are a Christian now too. God will bless you so much!"

Professor Don's decision to become a Christian made the wedding very special for all of us, but most of all for Professor Roley and Miss Penny. This was Mr. Jacko's legacy to his son, and to his daughter, and we all shared in the joy of it.

Isn't that just the blessing of God to His people? And I have told you so that you can enjoy the blessing too.

www.ingramcontent.com/pod-product-compliance
Ingram Content Group UK Ltd.
Pitfield, Milton Keynes, MK11 3LW, UK
UKHW020233250726
13967UKWH00001B/340

9 781471 661402